wild
Blessings

Weekly Devotions

for Boy Moms

ON THIS
Rock
SERIES

All Scriptures are taken from the THE HOLY BIBLE, ENGLISH STANDARD VERSION (ESV): Scriptures taken from THE HOLY BIBLE, ENGLISH STANDARD VERSION ® Copyright© 2001 by Crossway, a publishing ministry of Good News Publishers. Used by permission.

ISBN# 978-1-998532-43-8

1. Christianity 2. Devotions 3. Holy Bible 4. Parents

Printed in the United States of America
Published in the United States of America

support@aheliapublishing.org

Ahelia Publishing

I am a boy mom. I have been a boy mom for thirty-four years, and by the grace of God, my sons have all grown up to know and love Him. They are family men with kind hearts.

To expand slightly, I became a single mom to my boys when the youngest was only four. I understand the challenges and the heavy weight of responsibility that comes with it. But without the strength, wisdom, and mercy of Jesus, we'd never have made it.

But He is the answer. He has the answers. He gives grace when needed, strength when required, and peace, well, every day.

Raising boys is a joyous adventure, not for the faint of heart. They love mud, throwing things, wrestling, and getting as dirty as possible, even though they hate water unless they need it to make mud. Embrace their energy and zest for life, and you'll find the journey incredibly rewarding.

I pray you find something useful in each of these pages. I hope you use the suggestions and plan memorable activities with your boys. These are just some of the ones we found most fun.

Blessings to you, boy mom, as you raise God-fearing, emotionally healthy, kind young men. You got this because God's got you.

Kimm Reid

index

Behold, children are a heritage from the Lord, the fruit of the womb a reward.

Psalm 127:3

As A Boy Mom...

you are blessed with a unique journey filled with laughter, energy, and sometimes chaos. In the hustle and bustle of daily life, it's easy to forget the profound truth found in Psalm 127:3. Your sons are not merely children; they are a cherished heritage from the Lord, a reward that carries immense value and purpose.

Consider the word "heritage." It signifies a legacy, something of great worth passed down through generations. In the context of motherhood, it means that your role is integral to shaping your sons' lives and the future. Each moment you spend nurturing, teaching, and guiding them is a building block in the legacy of faith and love you are creating together.

Think about the challenges you face as a boy mom. Whether it's navigating the ups and downs of boys' energy, guiding them in being gentlemen, or even the difficulties of teaching them right from wrong, remember that these moments are significant.

Each challenge is an opportunity to instil values, share your faith, and show them the love of Christ, which are the cornerstones of all the other building blocks.

Praying for my Sons

Heavenly Father, thank You for the incredible gift of my sons. Help me to see them as the heritage You've entrusted to me. Grant me wisdom and patience as I guide them through life. May I always seek to reflect Your love and grace in our home and see them as the precious gifts from You. Amen.

Add your own personal prayer:

_____
_____
_____
_____
_____
_____
_____
_____
_____
_____
_____
_____
_____
_____
_____
_____
_____
_____
_____
_____
_____
_____
_____
_____

Make a Craft:
Collect items from a park, and create a craft together using the items.

Train up a child in the way he should go; even when he is old he will not depart from it.

Proverbs 22:6

As A Boy Mom...

you are entrusted with the incredible responsibility of shaping a young life. That life will grow up to be the head of a home, a breadwinner, a protector. This verse reminds us of the profound impact our guidance can have on our sons. Every conversation, every lesson, and every moment spent together is an opportunity to instill values that will last a lifetime.

Consider the ways you can actively train your son on the right path. This doesn't mean creating a perfect plan or expecting perfection. Instead, it's about being present and intentional in your interactions. Share your faith, model kindness, and encourage him to be strong and courageous, while forming it all within the understanding of healthy boundaries.

Reflect on the qualities you wish to nurture in your son. Is it compassion? Integrity? Resilience? Use everyday moments—during playtime, homework, or bedtime—to impart these lessons. Remember, training doesn't always happen in formal settings; it can be woven into the fabric of daily life.

Training up means purposeful conversation, but also playtime and silliness. It all builds a character that will last a lifetime.

Praying for my Sons

Dear Lord, thank you for the gift of my sons. Help me to be a wise and loving guide as I train him in your ways. Grant me patience and insight as I nurture his heart and mind. May he grow to be a man of integrity and faith, rooted in your love. Amen.

Add your own personal prayer:

_____
_____
_____
_____
_____
_____
_____
_____
_____
_____
_____
_____
_____
_____
_____
_____
_____
_____
_____
_____
_____
_____
_____

Write a Story Together:
Collaboratively write a short story.

But they who wait for the Lord shall renew their strength; they shall mount up with wings like eagles; they shall run and not be weary; they shall walk and not faint.

Isaiah 40:31

As A Boy Mom...

your days are often filled with energy, excitement, and sometimes exhaustion. Between playdates, school projects, and the endless questions from curious minds, it's easy to feel overwhelmed. Yet, Isaiah 40:31 offers a beautiful promise: those who wait on the Lord will find renewed strength.

This verse reminds us that we don't have to rely solely on our strength. Instead, we can turn to God, waiting on Him in prayer and reflection. In the busyness of motherhood, take moments to pause and seek His presence. Remember that He is ready to lift you up when you feel weary.

Think of the imagery of the eagle soaring high above the challenges below. God invites you to rise above the daily struggles to see your situation from His perspective. As you nurture and guide your boys, you can find the strength to tackle each challenge, knowing you are not alone.

Consider setting aside intentional time each day to connect with the Lord—whether through prayer, reading Scripture, or simply sitting in silence. Allow His strength to fill you so that you can pour love and energy into your sons.

Praying for my Sons

Heavenly Father, thank you for the promise of renewed strength. Help me to wait on You, especially during the challenging moments of motherhood. Fill me with Your power and peace, so I can be the strong and loving mom my boys need. May I soar like an eagle, trusting in Your provision and guidance. Amen.

Add your own personal prayer:

_____
_____
_____
_____
_____
_____
_____
_____
_____
_____
_____
_____
_____
_____
_____
_____
_____
_____
_____
_____
_____

Explore a new Restaurant.
Try a new cuisine together.

As A Boy Mom...

you play a crucial role in shaping the hearts and minds of your sons. Ephesians 6:4 reminds us of the balance between discipline and love. While it's important to instill boundaries and expectations, approaching this task can significantly impact our sons' emotional and spiritual growth.

This verse encourages us to nurture our children with patience and wisdom. It's a call to engage in their lives, guiding them through challenges while providing a safe space for them to express their feelings. Remember, discipline is not just about correction; it's about teaching—teaching them to make wise choices, set up appropriate boundaries, understand consequences, and grow in faith.

Reflect on your interactions with your boys. Are there moments when frustration takes over? When discipline feels more reactive than intentional? Take a step back and consider how to approach these situations gracefully. Use teachable moments to discuss values, reinforce love, and help them understand the "why" behind your guidance.

As you navigate the ups and downs of motherhood, lean on God for wisdom. Pray for the strength to be firm yet loving, to set boundaries while nurturing their hearts. Your boys will thrive in an environment where they know they are loved and understood.

Fathers, do not provoke your children to anger, but bring them up in the discipline and instruction of the Lord.

Ephesians 6:4

page 12

Praying for my Sons

Dear Lord, thank You for the gift of my sons. Help me to balance discipline and instruction with love and understanding. Grant me the patience to guide them in Your ways and the wisdom to create an environment where they feel safe to learn and grow. May my actions reflect Your love and grace in their lives. Amen.

Add your own personal prayer:

_____
_____
_____
_____
_____
_____
_____
_____
_____
_____
_____
_____
_____
_____
_____
_____
_____
_____
_____
_____
_____
_____

Visit a Library: Check out new books or attend a storytime.

As A Boy Mom...

your journey is filled with moments of joy, challenges, and countless prayers. Hannah's heartfelt declaration in 1 Samuel 1:27 is a poignant reminder of the power of prayer in motherhood. As Hannah earnestly prayed for her son Samuel, you, too, can bring your hopes, dreams, and concerns for your boys before the Lord.

This verse highlights the deep connection between a mother's heart and her child. Each day presents opportunities to pray for their well-being, character, and future. Whether for their safety, friendships, or spiritual growth, know that your prayers are powerful and meaningful.

Consider the moments when you feel overwhelmed or uncertain. Use these times to turn to God in prayer, just as Hannah did. Pour out your heart, expressing your fears and dreams for your sons. Trust that God hears your petitions and cares deeply for your children.

As you nurture and guide your boys, remember to celebrate the answered prayers in your life. Reflect on how God has worked in their lives and express gratitude for His faithfulness. These moments of thankfulness can strengthen your faith and deepen your bond with your children.

For this child I prayed, and the Lord has granted me my petition that I made to him.

1 Samuel 1:27

Praying for my Sons

Heavenly Father, thank You for the precious gift of my sons. Help me to be diligent in prayer, bringing my hopes and concerns before You. Grant me the wisdom to guide them and the faith to trust in Your plans for their lives. May I always celebrate Your faithfulness and love in our journey together. Amen.

Add your own personal prayer:

_____
_____
_____
_____
_____
_____
_____
_____
_____
_____
_____
_____
_____
_____
_____
_____
_____
_____
_____
_____
_____
_____

Indoor Obstacle Course: Create a fun course using furniture and toys.

And these words that I command you today shall be on your heart. You shall teach them diligently to your children...

Deut.
6:6-7

As A Boy Mom...

you have a unique opportunity to weave faith into the fabric of your everyday life. Deuteronomy 6:6-7 encourages us to make God's words a central part of our daily conversations and interactions with our children. This isn't about formal lessons; it's about integrating faith into the rhythm of your lives.

Think about the moments you share with your sons—during meal times, car rides, or bedtime routines. Each of these times can be transformed into opportunities for discussions about God's love, His promises, and the values you want to instill in them. Share stories from the Bible, reflect on what you're grateful for, or discuss how to navigate challenges with faith.

Consider how you can model a life of faith for your boys. Your actions speak volumes. Let them see you praying, reading Scripture, and living out your beliefs in your choices and attitudes. This modeling will leave a lasting impression on their hearts and minds.

Remember, teaching isn't just about imparting knowledge; it's about nurturing a relationship with God that your sons can embrace as they grow. As you engage in these conversations, pray for God to guide your words and to help you create an environment where faith flourishes.

Praying for my Sons

Lord, thank You for the blessing of my sons. Help me to teach them Your ways in every moment we share. May Your words be on my heart, and may I be intentional in guiding them toward a deeper relationship with You. Give me the wisdom to turn everyday moments into opportunities for spiritual growth. Amen.

Add your own personal prayer:

_____
_____
_____
_____
_____
_____
_____
_____
_____
_____
_____
_____
_____
_____
_____
_____
_____
_____
_____
_____
_____
_____

Cook Breakfast Together: make pancakes or omelets as a team.

As A Boy Mom...

you often face unique challenges and decisions that can feel overwhelming. From navigating school issues to guiding your sons through growing pains, the journey of motherhood is filled with moments that require wisdom. James 1:5 offers a beautiful promise: when we lack wisdom, we can ask God, and He will provide it generously.

In the hustle and bustle of daily life, it's easy to rely on our instincts or seek advice from friends. While there's value in the community, remember that God is the ultimate source of wisdom. He knows your sons intimately and understands their needs, fears, and aspirations better than anyone else—including you.

Make it a practice to bring your concerns and questions before the Lord. Whether you're unsure how to address a particular behavior or how to support them during a tough time, take a moment to pray and ask for guidance. Trust that God will help you navigate these situations and give you the insights you need.

As you seek His wisdom, remain open to how He may speak to you—through Scripture, a conversation, or a quiet moment of reflection. Embrace the journey of learning and growing alongside your boys, knowing you are not alone.

If any of you lacks wisdom, let him ask of God, who gives generously to all without reproach, and it will be given him.

James 1:5

Praying for my Sons

Heavenly Father, thank You for the gift of my sons. I ask for Your wisdom as I guide and nurture them. Help me to seek Your counsel in every decision I face, and grant me clarity and insight. May I trust in Your generous provision of wisdom as I navigate the challenges of motherhood. Amen.

Add your own personal prayer:

_____
_____
_____
_____
_____
_____
_____
_____
_____
_____
_____
_____
_____
_____
_____
_____
_____
_____
_____
_____
_____
_____
_____

DIY Tie-Dye T-Shirts: Use fabric dye to create colorful shirts.

As A Boy Mom...

your days are often filled with a whirlwind of activities, challenges, and responsibilities. From managing school projects to navigating emotional ups and downs, feeling overwhelmed is easy. Yet, Philippians 4:13 reminds us that we are not alone in these struggles; we draw strength from Christ.

This verse powerfully affirms that you can face any challenge with confidence. Whether you're tackling a difficult conversation with your son or balancing various demands on your time, remember that Christ equips you with the strength you need. His power is made perfect in your weakness, enabling you to rise to the occasion.

Reflect on the moments when you feel inadequate or unsure. In those times, pause and remind yourself of this promise. Lean into prayer, asking God to fill you with His strength and wisdom. He is ready to empower you to handle whatever comes your way.

As you nurture your boys, let them see you relying on this strength. Share with them how faith can transform challenges into opportunities for growth. Teaching them to lean on Christ in their lives will instill resilience and confidence in their hearts.

I can do all things through him who strengthens me.

Phil 4:13

Praying for my Sons

Lord, thank You for the strength You provide in every situation. Help me to trust in You as I navigate the challenges of motherhood. May I model reliance on Your power for my sons, teaching them to find their strength in You as well. Equip me to be the mom they need, filled with Your grace and courage. Amen.

Add your own personal prayer:

_____
_____
_____
_____
_____
_____
_____
_____
_____
_____
_____
_____
_____
_____
_____
_____
_____
_____
_____
_____
_____
_____

Scavenger Hunt: Create a list of items to find in your backyard or park.

As A Boy Mom...

you play a vital role in shaping your sons' hearts and minds. Colossians 3:21 reminds us of the importance of nurturing our children with love and encouragement rather than provoking them to frustration. This verse is a gentle reminder to cultivate a positive and supportive environment for your boys.

Encourage your sons to express their thoughts and feelings openly, knowing they are heard and valued. Create opportunities for open dialogue where they can share their challenges and triumphs without fear of judgment. This fosters trust and strengthens your bond.

Model kindness in your interactions with them. Recognize the pressures they face and be mindful of your words and actions. Instead of criticism, focus on constructive feedback that encourages growth and resilience. Celebrate their efforts and achievements, no matter how small, reinforcing their self-worth and confidence.

Help them understand that mistakes are a natural part of learning. Teach them to approach challenges with a growth mindset, knowing that God loves them unconditionally and is always there to guide them through difficult times.

By emphasizing encouragement and kindness, you create a safe space for your sons to thrive, equipping them to face the world with courage and faith.

Fathers, do not provoke your children, lest they become discouraged.

Colossians 3:21

Praying for my Sons

Dear Lord, thank You for my sons and the privilege of guiding them. Help me to encourage and nurture their hearts, avoiding words or actions that may discourage them. May our home be filled with love, support, and understanding as we grow together in faith. Strengthen our family bond and help us reflect Your kindness in all we do. Amen.

Add your own personal prayer:

_____
_____
_____
_____
_____
_____
_____
_____
_____
_____
_____
_____
_____
_____
_____
_____
_____
_____
_____
_____
_____

Have a Themed Dinner Night: Choose a theme and cook accordingly.

As A Boy Mom...

you often find yourself faced with decisions that can feel overwhelming. Whether choosing the right school, guiding them through friendships, or helping them navigate their emotions, it's natural to rely on your understanding. Yet, Proverbs 3:5-6 invites you to place your trust entirely in the Lord.

Trusting God means surrendering your worries and fears to Him, knowing He is aware and has a perfect plan. It's a reminder that while you may not always have clarity or answers, God does. When you acknowledge Him in every aspect of motherhood—big or small—He promises to guide your steps.

Consider how you can intentionally practice trust in your daily life. When challenges arise, take a moment to pray and seek God's wisdom. Reflect on past experiences where trusting Him led to unexpected blessings or clarity. These reminders can strengthen your faith and encourage you to lean on Him fully.

As you navigate the ups and downs of raising your boys, model this trust for them. Share with them how faith plays a role in your decisions and encourages you during tough times. Teach them the importance of seeking God's guidance in their own lives.

Trust in the Lord with all your heart, and do not lean on your own understanding. In all your ways acknowledge him, and he will make straight your paths.

Proverbs 3:5-6

Praying for my Sons

Dear Lord, thank You for the promise of Your guidance. Help me to trust You with all my heart as I navigate the challenges of motherhood. May I lean on You instead of my own understanding and acknowledge You in all my ways. Guide my steps and help me instill this trust in my sons as they grow. Amen.

Add your own personal prayer:

_____
_____
_____
_____
_____
_____
_____
_____
_____
_____
_____
_____
_____
_____
_____
_____
_____
_____
_____
_____
_____
_____

Take a Day Trip: Visit a nearby city or attraction.

As A Boy Mom...

your heart is often filled with love and concern for your sons. You want to protect them from harm, guide them in their decisions, and ensure they grow into strong, faithful individuals. Psalm 34:7 offers a beautiful reminder that God is our ultimate protector. His angels encamp around those who honor Him, providing safety and deliverance.

Remember that God is actively watching over them in moments of worry—whether it's about their safety, friendships, or future. He knows their hearts and challenges, and He is committed to their well-being. This verse encourages you to instill in your boys a reverence for God, teaching them to rely on Him as their protector.

Take time to pray for your sons, asking God to surround them with His angels. Encourage them to seek God's presence in their lives, reminding them that they are never alone. This foundation of faith will give them security and empower them to face life's challenges with courage.

As you reflect on this promise, let it strengthen your resolve to trust God's protection. Share stories of how God has been faithful in your life and shown His care over your family.

The angel of the Lord encamps around those who fear him, and delivers them.

Psalm 34:7

Praying for my Sons

Heavenly Father, thank You for the assurance that You protect my sons. Help me to teach them to honor You and trust in Your deliverance. May Your angels surround them in all they do, and may I find peace in knowing You are their ultimate guardian. Guide my heart as I nurture their faith and security in You. Amen.

Add your own personal prayer:

_____
_____
_____
_____
_____
_____
_____
_____
_____
_____
_____
_____
_____
_____
_____
_____
_____
_____
_____
_____
_____
_____

Swimming: Go to a pool or local swimming spot.

As A Boy Mom...

you play a vital role in shaping the character and faith of your sons. In 1 Corinthians 16:13, Paul encourages believers to be watchful, stand firm in their faith, and act with strength. This call is significant for you as you guide your boys into manhood.

Teaching your sons to be watchful means helping them develop discernment in a world filled with distractions and challenges. Encourage them to stay alert to the influences around them, both positive and negative. This vigilance will empower them to make wise choices and cultivate a strong moral compass.

Standing firm in faith requires you to model what it means to trust God, even amidst uncertainty. Share with your boys the importance of relying on Scripture and prayer as they navigate their journeys. Remind them that true strength comes from a deep relationship with God, which will help them face life's trials with courage.

Finally, encourage them to act like men—not just in physical strength but in character, integrity, and kindness. Discuss what it means to be strong in their faith and to support one another as brothers. This foundation will not only help them grow individually but also foster a supportive bond between them.

Be watchful, stand firm in the faith, act like men, be strong.

1 Cor. 16:13

Praying for my Sons

Lord, thank You for the privilege of raising my sons. Help me to teach them to be watchful and to stand firm in their faith. May they grow in strength and character, reflecting Your love and truth in their lives. Equip me to be a guiding light as they learn what it means to act with courage and integrity. Amen.

Add your own personal prayer:

_____
_____
_____
_____
_____
_____
_____
_____
_____
_____
_____
_____
_____
_____
_____
_____
_____
_____
_____
_____
_____
_____
_____
_____
_____

Science Experiments: Try simple experiments at home.

As A Boy Mom...

you have the incredible opportunity to impart wisdom and guidance to your sons. Proverbs 1:8-9 emphasizes the importance of both parental instruction and teaching, highlighting how these lessons can adorn their lives like a beautiful garland.

Your role is vital in helping your boys navigate the complexities of life. Teaching them to value your guidance means encouraging them to listen and learn from your experiences. Share your insights on faith, integrity, and decision-making, and remind them that your teachings are rooted in love and care.

These verses also remind us of the beauty that wisdom brings. Just as a garland adorns the head, your teachings can enrich their lives, giving them strength and direction. Encourage your sons to embrace wisdom from you and Scripture as they grow and face new challenges.

As they learn to appreciate the value of your guidance, you are helping to cultivate their character and equip them for the future. Reinforce the idea that wisdom is a treasure that will serve them well throughout their lives.

Hear, my son, your father's instruction, and forsake not your mother's teaching, for they are a graceful garland for your head and pendants for your neck.

Proverbs 1:8-9

Praying for my Sons

Dear Lord, thank You for the gift of my sons. Help me to teach them with love and patience, instilling in them a desire to seek wisdom. May my guidance be like a beautiful garland in their lives, leading them closer to You. Give me the words to share and the grace to nurture their hearts. Amen.

Add your own personal prayer:

_____
_____
_____
_____
_____
_____
_____
_____
_____
_____
_____
_____
_____
_____
_____
_____
_____
_____
_____
_____
_____
_____
_____

Karaoke night: Sing along to favorite songs at home.

As A Boy Mom...

you have a unique role in guiding your sons toward a relationship with Jesus. In Matthew 19:14, we see Jesus welcoming children with open arms, emphasizing their importance in the Kingdom of Heaven. This verse serves as a beautiful reminder of the value God places on the hearts of children and the significance of nurturing their faith.

Your boys are at a stage where they are curious and impressionable. This is the perfect time to encourage them to approach Jesus with their questions, fears, and joys. Create an environment where faith is a natural part of your daily life—through prayer, Bible stories, and open discussions about their feelings and experiences.

Consider how you can model Christ-like love and acceptance in your home. Show them that Jesus is not just a figure from stories but a friend who cares deeply for them. Encourage them to come to Him in prayer, teaching them that they can share anything with Him.

As you guide your sons, remind them of the importance of kindness, compassion, and faithfulness—qualities that reflect Jesus's heart. Help them understand that they are cherished in God's eyes and that their relationship with Him will give them strength and purpose.

But Jesus said, 'Let the little children come to me and do not hinder them, for to such belongs the kingdom of heaven.

Matthew 19:14

Praying for my Sons

Lord, thank You for my sons and the gift of their innocence. Help me to guide them toward You, showing them the beauty of coming to Jesus. May our home be a place where faith flourishes, and may I nurture their hearts to seek You in all things. Teach me to model Your love and acceptance, so they may grow in faith and confidence. Amen.

Add your own personal prayer:

Design your Own Sandwiches: Use various ingredients to build fun sandwiches.

As A Boy Mom...

you are entrusted with the precious responsibility of raising your sons in a world of many challenges and distractions. Isaiah 54:13 offers a comforting promise: when we guide our children to God, He will teach them, and they will experience profound peace.

This verse reminds us of the importance of instilling a love for God in our children. Your role in their lives is to provide for their physical needs and nurture their spiritual growth. Encourage your boys to seek the Lord through prayer, Scripture, and genuine conversations about faith. Create opportunities for them to experience God's presence through family devotions, exploring nature, or serving others.

When your sons are taught by the Lord, they gain wisdom and peace that surpasses any struggles they may face. Teach them true peace comes from trusting God, even when life gets tough. Share stories of how your faith has comforted you during challenging times, helping them see the relevance of faith in everyday life.

As you guide them, remember that your influence is significant. Your prayers and teachings can shape their understanding of who God is and how much they are loved.

All your children shall be taught by the Lord, and great shall be the peace of your children.

Isaiah 54:13

Praying for my Sons

Heavenly Father, thank You for the gift of my sons. Help me to lead them close to You, instilling in them a love for Your Word and a desire to know You. May they experience the peace that comes from being taught by You, fill their hearts with Your wisdom. Guide me as I nurture their faith, so they grow to be strong and confident in Your love. Amen.

Add your own personal prayer:

_____
_____
_____
_____
_____
_____
_____
_____
_____
_____
_____
_____
_____
_____
_____
_____
_____
_____
_____
_____
_____
_____
_____
_____

Stargazing: Lay out a blanket and watch the stars at night.

As A Boy Mom...

you navigate the joys and challenges of parenting daily, often wondering how to guide your sons on the right path. Psalm 119:105 offers a comforting assurance that God's Word provides direction and clarity, illuminating the way ahead.

In a world filled with choices and distractions, the Bible is essential for teaching your boys about values, integrity, and faith. Encourage them to see Scripture not just as stories but as a guiding light that can help them make wise decisions. Whether they face peer pressure, academic challenges, or personal struggles, remind them that God's Word can provide the wisdom they need.

Incorporate daily moments to explore the Bible together. Share stories that resonate with their experiences and discuss how these lessons apply to their lives. Create a routine of family devotions, allowing them to see the importance of seeking God's guidance in all things.

As they learn to rely on God's Word, they will gain confidence in their ability to navigate life's paths. Teach them that while they may not always see the entire journey ahead, trusting in God's light will help them take each step with faith.

Your word is a lamp to my feet and a light to my path.

Psalm 119:105

Praying for my Sons

Lord, thank You for the gift of Your Word, which guides us through life. Help me to instill in my sons a love for Scripture and a desire to seek Your wisdom. May Your Word illuminate their paths, providing clarity and strength as they grow. Teach them to trust in You, knowing that You are always with them. Amen.

Add your own personal prayer:

_____
_____
_____
_____
_____
_____
_____
_____
_____
_____
_____
_____
_____
_____
_____
_____
_____
_____
_____
_____
_____
_____
_____
_____

Play with Pets:
Spend time playing with family pets or visit a pet store.

As A Boy Mom...

you play a crucial role in shaping the character and values of your sons. Proverbs 4:7 reminds us that wisdom is the foundation upon which we build our lives. It encourages us to prioritize gaining wisdom and insight above all else, a powerful message to impart to your boys.

From an early age, teach your sons that wisdom is not just about knowledge but about understanding how to apply it in their lives. Encourage them to ask questions, explore, and seek out truth. Share with them the importance of listening—to others and to the guidance of the Holy Spirit.

Create an environment where learning is valued. Discuss real-life situations and the lessons that can be learned from them. Encourage them to reflect on their choices and the consequences that follow, helping them see that wisdom often comes from experience and thoughtful consideration.

As your boys grow, remind them that seeking wisdom is a lifelong journey. Encourage them to turn to Scripture for guidance and to seek counsel from trusted mentors and role models. By instilling this value in them, you are equipping them to make wise decisions and confidently navigate life's challenges.

The beginning of wisdom is this: Get wisdom, and whatever you get, get insight.

Proverbs 4:7

Praying for my Sons

Dear Lord, thank You for the gift of wisdom. Help me to nurture a love for learning in my sons and to guide them in seeking understanding. May they recognize the importance of wisdom in their lives and learn to apply it in all they do. Equip me to be a wise mentor, leading them closer to You. Amen.

Add your own personal prayer:

_____
_____
_____
_____
_____
_____
_____
_____
_____
_____
_____
_____
_____
_____
_____
_____
_____
_____
_____
_____
_____
_____
_____

Learn a new Dance:
Follow online dance tutorials together.

But the fruit of the Spirit is love, joy, peace, patience, kindness, goodness, faithfulness, gentleness, self-control...

Galatians
5:22-23

As A Boy Mom...

you have the unique opportunity to nurture the character of your sons and help them understand the importance of the fruits of the Spirit. In Galatians 5:22-23, Paul outlines these virtues that reflect a life led by the Holy Spirit, offering a beautiful framework for building their character.

Start by modeling these qualities in your own life. Show them what it means to love unconditionally, to express joy in everyday moments, and to seek peace in conflicts. Your actions will speak volumes, teaching them that these virtues are not just words but essential parts of a fulfilling life.

Encourage your boys to practice patience, especially in their interactions with others. Remind them that self-control is a strength, helping them make wise choices even when faced with temptation. Engage in discussions about kindness and goodness, helping them understand the impact of their actions on those around them.

Create opportunities for them to serve others, reinforcing that expressing love and kindness is vital to their faith. Celebrate the moments when they exhibit these fruits, acknowledging their growth and encouraging them to continue developing these qualities.

As they learn to embrace the fruits of the Spirit, they will grow in character and strengthen their relationships with God and with others.

Praying for my Sons

Heavenly Father, thank You for the fruits of the Spirit that guide us in our daily lives. Help me to model these qualities for my sons and to encourage them to cultivate love, joy, peace, and patience. May they grow in kindness and self-control, reflecting Your light in the world. Equip me to nurture their hearts as they learn to walk in Your ways. Amen.

Add your own personal prayer:

_____
_____
_____
_____
_____
_____
_____
_____
_____
_____
_____
_____
_____
_____
_____
_____
_____
_____
_____
_____
_____
_____
_____

Attend a Local Fair or Festival: Enjoy rides, games, and food.

As A Boy Mom...

instilling a reverent fear of the Lord in your sons is one of the greatest gifts you can give them. Psalm 112:1 beautifully illustrates the blessings that come to those who honor God and take joy in His commandments. This verse serves as a reminder of a faith-filled life's profound impact on your family.

Teach your boys that fearing the Lord is not about being afraid but recognizing His greatness and authority. Help them understand that true wisdom begins with a heart that seeks to honor God. Encourage them to delight in His Word, exploring the richness of His commandments and how they guide us toward a fulfilling life.

Create moments in your daily routine to discuss the importance of following God's ways. Share stories from your life where obeying God's commands brought blessings or taught valuable lessons. Encourage them to see that delighting in God's law leads to joy, peace, and a purposeful life.

As your sons grow in their understanding of God's love and His commandments, they will learn to navigate life's challenges with faith and integrity. Your guidance will help them cultivate a heart that not only fears the Lord but also delights in living out His truth.

Praise the Lord! Blessed is the man who fears the Lord, who greatly delights in his commandments!

Psalm 112:1

Praying for my Sons

Lord, thank You for the blessings that come from fearing You and delighting in Your commandments. Help me to teach my sons the importance of honoring You in all they do. May their hearts be filled with reverence and joy as they seek to follow Your ways. Guide me as I model a life rooted in faith, so they may grow to love You deeply. Amen.

Add your own personal prayer:

_____
_____
_____
_____
_____
_____
_____
_____
_____
_____
_____
_____
_____
_____
_____
_____
_____
_____
_____
_____
_____
_____

mini golf:
Visit a mini-golf course for some fun.

A soft answer turns away wrath, but a harsh word stirs up anger.

Proverbs 15:1

As A Boy Mom...

you know that the dynamics of raising boys can be lively and sometimes tumultuous. Proverbs 15:1 offers a profound insight into the power of our words, reminding us that a gentle response can diffuse tension and promote understanding.

In the heat of the moment—whether it's a disagreement with a sibling or frustration with homework—encourage your sons to think before they speak. Help them practice responding with kindness and patience, showing them that their words can either build up or tear down. Teach them that a soft answer not only reflects their character but also has the potential to transform a situation.

Model this behavior yourself. Responding with grace and composure when challenges arise demonstrates how a gentle tone can create a peaceful environment. Share stories of times when you chose kindness over frustration and the positive outcomes that followed.

Create opportunities for your boys to practice this principle. Role-playing different scenarios can help them understand how to respond with gentleness in real-life situations. Reinforce the idea that their words hold power and that they can choose to be peacemakers in their interactions.

By nurturing this skill, you equip your sons to approach conflicts with love and wisdom, fostering healthy relationships throughout their lives.

Praying for my Sons

Dear Lord, thank You for the wisdom found in Your Word. Help me to teach my sons the importance of gentle words and kind responses. May they learn to navigate their relationships with love and patience, reflecting Your grace in their interactions. Guide us in creating a home filled with understanding and peace. Amen.

Add your own personal prayer:

_____
_____
_____
_____
_____
_____
_____
_____
_____
_____
_____
_____
_____
_____
_____
_____
_____
_____
_____
_____
_____
_____
_____
_____

Read Together: Choose a book to read aloud and discuss.

I am reminded of your sincere faith, a faith that dwelt first in your grandmother Lois and your mother Eunice...

2 Timothy 1:5

As A Boy Mom...

you have the incredible opportunity to pass down a legacy of faith to your sons, just as Timothy received from his grandmother and mother. In 2 Timothy 1:5, Paul highlights the importance of sincere faith nurtured within the family. This verse is a powerful reminder of the impact you can have on your children's spiritual journey.

Consider the faith that you model in your everyday life. Your boys watch how you navigate challenges, express gratitude, and seek God in all circumstances. Be intentional about sharing your faith stories, including the struggles and victories that have shaped your relationship with Christ. This openness can inspire them and help them see the relevance of faith in their own lives.

Encourage your sons to ask questions about faith, fostering an environment where they feel comfortable exploring their beliefs. Engage in family devotions, prayer times, and discussions about Scripture, making faith a natural part of your family's daily rhythm.

Remember that your influence is profound. Just as Lois and Eunice laid the foundation for Timothy's faith, your love, guidance, and example can help your boys grow into men of God. Pray for them regularly, asking the Lord to cultivate a deep and sincere faith in their hearts.

Praying for my Sons

Heavenly Father, thank You for the gift of faith that has been passed down through generations. Help me to nurture this legacy in my sons, instilling in them a sincere love for You. May they grow to be strong in their faith, drawing on the examples of those who have gone before them. Guide me as I lead them in Your ways. Amen.

Add your own personal prayer:

_____
_____
_____
_____
_____
_____
_____
_____
_____
_____
_____
_____
_____
_____
_____
_____
_____
_____
_____
_____
_____
_____

Puzzle Time:
Work on a jigsaw puzzle together.

As A Boy Mom...

you understand the importance of instilling values in your sons that will guide them throughout their lives. Psalm 119:11 emphasizes the significance of internalizing God's Word, reminding us that we are better equipped to navigate life's challenges and temptations when we hide His teachings in our hearts.

Encourage your boys to develop a habit of memorizing Scripture. Help them see that God's Word is not just for Sunday mornings but is a source of strength, wisdom, and guidance in their daily lives. Consider creating fun and engaging ways to memorize verses together—through songs, games, or even crafts. This can make the process enjoyable and meaningful.

Share stories from your life where Scripture has helped you make wise choices or comfort you in difficult times. Let them know that the more they know God's Word, the more it will influence their thoughts and actions.

Establish family devotion times where you read the Bible together, discuss its meaning, and explore how it applies to your lives. This will not only teach them the importance of Scripture but also create a bond centered around faith.

As your sons grow and face life's challenges, having the Word of God stored in their hearts will serve as a powerful guide, leading them toward righteousness and helping them resist temptation.

I have stored up your word in my heart, that I might not sin against you.

Psalm 119:11

Praying for my Sons

Dear Lord, thank You for the treasure of Your Word. Help me to encourage my sons to hide Your teachings in their hearts. May they find strength and guidance in Scripture as they grow, helping them to live in a way that honors You. Guide us as we seek to make Your Word a central part of our lives. Amen.

Add your own personal prayer:

_____
_____
_____
_____
_____
_____
_____
_____
_____
_____
_____
_____
_____
_____
_____
_____
_____
_____
_____
_____
_____
_____

Create Smoothies: Experiment with different fruit combinations.

Therefore, since we are surrounded by so great a cloud of witnesses, let us also lay aside every weight...

Hebrews 12:1

As A Boy Mom...

you have the privilege of guiding your sons in their faith journey, teaching them to run the race of life with purpose and perseverance. Hebrews 12:1 invites us to consider the great cloud of witnesses who have gone before us, reminding us that we are not alone in our struggles and triumphs.

Encourage your boys to be aware of the legacy of faith surrounding them—their family, friends, and heroes of faith who have paved the way. Share stories of individuals who have overcome challenges through their faith, showing them that they can face obstacles with courage and determination.

Help them understand the importance of shedding anything that hinders their spiritual growth. Discuss the "weights" in their lives—distractions, fears, negative influences, or unhealthy habits—and how to let go of those things to stay focused on their goals.

Create a culture of encouragement in your home where they feel supported to pursue their dreams and passions. Celebrate their achievements, no matter how small, and remind them that each step they take in faith is significant.

As they learn to run their race with endurance, guide them to look to Jesus, the author and perfecter of their faith. Encourage them to pray and seek His guidance, knowing that He is always with them, cheering them on.

Praying for my Sons

Heavenly Father, thank You for the race of faith that You have set before us. Help me to teach my sons to run with endurance, laying aside anything that hinders them. May they be inspired by the witnesses of faith around them and look to Jesus as their guide. Strengthen them in their journey, and may they always seek to honor You in all they do. Amen.

Add your own personal prayer:

_____
_____
_____
_____
_____
_____
_____
_____
_____
_____
_____
_____
_____
_____
_____
_____
_____
_____
_____
_____

Build a Fort: Use blankets and pillows to create a cozy fort.

As A Boy Mom...

life can sometimes feel overwhelming. Between school activities, friendships, and the everyday challenges of raising boys, it's easy to feel weighed down by worries and anxieties. In 1 Peter 5:7, we are reminded of the beautiful truth that we can cast all our cares on God because He genuinely cares for us.

Teach your sons the importance of handing over their worries to God. Help them understand that it's okay to feel anxious or uncertain but that they don't have to carry those burdens alone. Encourage them to have open conversations about their fears and concerns, creating a safe space for them to express their feelings.

Share with them the practical ways to cast their anxieties on God—through prayer, journaling, or even simply talking about their worries. Model this behavior in your own life. When you face challenges, demonstrate how you turn to God in prayer, showing them that reliance on Him is a source of strength.

Remind your boys that God cares for them deeply and desires to help them through their struggles. Encourage them to reflect on how God has supported them in the past, reinforcing that He is always faithful.

As they learn to cast their cares on Him, they will grow in trust and faith, understanding that they are never alone in their journey.

Casting all your anxieties on him, because he cares for you.

1 Peter 5:7

Praying for my Sons

Dear Lord, thank You for inviting us to cast our anxieties on You. Help me to teach my sons to rely on You in times of worry and uncertainty. May they feel Your love and care in their lives, learning to trust You with all their hearts. Guide us as we navigate the challenges of life together, knowing that we can always turn to You. Amen.

Add your own personal prayer:

_____
_____
_____
_____
_____
_____
_____
_____
_____
_____
_____
_____
_____
_____
_____
_____
_____
_____
_____
_____
_____
_____

Picnic in the Park:
Pack lunch and enjoy it outdoors.

As A Boy Mom...

you often find yourself navigating the ups and downs of raising energetic and spirited boys. Exodus 14:14 provides a powerful reminder of God's promise to fight for us in moments of challenge or uncertainty. This verse encourages us to trust in His protection and guidance, especially when we feel overwhelmed.

Teach your sons that there will be times when they face difficulties—whether it's a tough situation at school, a conflict with friends, or even their own fears. Remind them that they can rely on God to be their defender in these moments. Help them understand that the best action is to be still and trust God is at work.

Encourage them to pray when they feel anxious or uncertain. Show them how to surrender their worries to God, affirming that He is bigger than any problem they face. Share stories of seeing God intervene in your life, highlighting times when you felt helpless yet watched Him work wonders.

Create a family culture where faith and trust in God are discussed openly. Share Scripture together, focusing on how God fights for us and provides for our needs. As they grow in their understanding of His faithfulness, they will learn to stand firm in the face of adversity. By instilling this lesson, you equip your boys to approach challenges confidently, knowing they are supported by a loving and powerful God.

The Lord will fight for you, and you have only to be silent.

Exodus 14:14

Praying for my Sons

Heavenly Father, thank You for the promise that You will fight for us. Help me teach my sons to trust in Your protection and to be still in the face of their challenges. May they learn to turn to You in prayer and find peace in knowing that You are always with them. Guide us as we navigate life's battles together, trusting in Your faithfulness. Amen.

Add your own personal prayer:

_____
_____
_____
_____
_____
_____
_____
_____
_____
_____
_____
_____
_____
_____
_____
_____
_____
_____
_____
_____
_____
_____
_____

Do a Family Project: Work together on a home improvement task.

May the God of hope fill you with all joy and peace in believing...

Romans 15:13

As A Boy Mom...

you often find yourself in the midst of energetic adventures and challenges. Romans 15:13 offers a beautiful reminder that God is the source of hope, joy, and peace. This verse encourages us to lean into our faith and trust in God's promises in a world that can sometimes feel uncertain.

Teach your sons about the importance of hope and how it can shape their outlook on life. Help them understand that hope is not just wishful thinking but a confident expectation rooted in God's character. Share with them how your faith in God has brought you joy and peace, even during tough times.

Encourage them to seek God in prayer when they feel discouraged or anxious. Remind them that the Holy Spirit empowers us to experience a deep sense of hope, even when circumstances seem challenging. Create family rituals that foster an atmosphere of hope, such as sharing what you're thankful for or discussing how God has been faithful in your lives.

As they grow, instill in them the belief that they can also be sources of hope for others. Encourage kindness, support, and encouragement toward their friends and family. Teach them that by sharing their hope in Christ, they can positively impact those around them.

By nurturing a spirit of hope in your home, you equip your boys to face life's ups and downs confidently, knowing that God is always with them.

Praying for my Sons

Dear Lord, thank You for being the God of hope. Fill my sons with joy and peace as they believe in You. Help us to trust in Your promises and share that hope with others. May Your Holy Spirit empower them to be beacons of hope in a world that needs it. Guide us as we walk in faith together. Amen.

Add your own personal prayer:

_____
_____
_____
_____
_____
_____
_____
_____
_____
_____
_____
_____
_____
_____
_____
_____
_____
_____
_____
_____
_____

Attend a Live Performance:
Check out a play or concert.

As A Boy Mom...

life can be filled with unpredictable moments—joyful adventures, unexpected challenges, and everything in between. Psalm 46:1 reassures us that God is our refuge and strength, always available to help us in times of trouble. This promise is a powerful reminder that we are never alone in our parenting journey.

Teach your sons about the importance of seeking refuge in God during difficult times. Help them understand that feeling overwhelmed or scared is okay, but they can always turn to God for comfort and strength. Encourage open discussions about their feelings, creating a safe space for them to express their concerns.

Share stories from your own life where you experienced God's help during challenging situations. Whether it was a moment of fear, stress, or uncertainty, recount how turning to prayer or Scripture provided you with peace and guidance. This modeling shows them that reliance on God is both practical and powerful.

In times of stress, teach them simple prayers or verses they can recite to remind themselves of God's presence. Establish family rituals, like a nightly prayer or a gratitude moment, to reinforce the idea that God is always there to support and strengthen you.

By instilling this understanding, you equip your boys to face challenges confidently, knowing they can find refuge in God's loving arms.

God is our refuge and strength, a very present help in trouble.

Psalm 46:1

Praying for my Sons

Heavenly Father, thank You for being our refuge and strength. Help me teach my sons to turn to You in times of trouble, knowing that You are always present to help. May they find comfort in Your love and strength in their faith. Guide us as we navigate life's challenges together, trusting in Your unfailing support. Amen.

Add your own personal prayer:

_____
_____
_____
_____
_____
_____
_____
_____
_____
_____
_____
_____
_____
_____
_____
_____
_____
_____
_____
_____
_____
_____

Go Hiking: Explore nearby trails and enjoy nature.

As A Boy Mom...

you have the incredible opportunity to teach your sons about the power of love—both in how they receive and give it. 1 John 4:19 reminds us that our ability to love others comes from understanding and experiencing God's love for us. This foundational truth can shape their interactions with family, friends, and the world around them.

Encourage your boys to reflect on how God has shown His love in their lives. Share stories of love and kindness you've experienced, emphasizing how these moments reflect God's heart for us. Help them understand that love is not just an emotion but an action they can express daily.

Teach them to love others, especially those who may be challenging to love. Discuss practical ways to show kindness—through words of encouragement, acts of service, or simply being a good friend. Reinforce the idea that loving others is a response to the love they have received from God.

Create a family culture that prioritizes love and compassion. Celebrate moments when your sons show love to others, no matter how small. Let them know that their actions reflect God's love and make a difference in the lives of those around them.

By instilling this understanding, you nurture their hearts to be filled with love, preparing them to be compassionate individuals who mirror God's love in a world that needs it.

We love because he first loved us.

1 John 4:19

Praying for my Sons

Dear Lord, thank You for loving us first and teaching us how to love. Help me guide my sons in understanding and expressing Your love in their lives. May they grow to be compassionate and kind, reflecting Your love to everyone they encounter. Strengthen us as a family to live out this love daily. Amen.

Add your own personal prayer:

_____
_____
_____
_____
_____
_____
_____
_____
_____
_____
_____
_____
_____
_____
_____
_____
_____
_____
_____
_____
_____
_____

Attend a local sporting game together.

As A Boy Mom...

you quickly realize that life is a beautiful tapestry of seasons—some joyful, some challenging, and all unique, especially with a houseful of boys. Ecclesiastes 3:1 reminds us that each moment has its purpose, encouraging us to embrace the different phases of life with grace and understanding.

Teach your sons that just as nature has its seasons, so do their lives. Help them recognize that it's normal to experience various emotions and circumstances. Whether they're enjoying carefree days of play or facing the struggles of growing up, each season brings valuable lessons and opportunities for growth.

Encourage them to appreciate the present moment. Share with them the importance of being fully present, whether they are having fun with friends or navigating tough times. Discuss how God uses every experience to shape their character and faith, reminding them that even difficult seasons can lead to growth and deeper understanding.

Create family traditions that honor different seasons—celebrating milestones, reflecting on lessons learned, and cherishing the time spent together. These moments foster gratitude and help your boys see the beauty in both the joyful and challenging times of life.

By instilling this perspective, you equip your sons to approach life's changes confidently, knowing that God is with them through every season.

For everything there is a season, and a time for every matter under heaven.

Eccles. 3:1

Praying for my Sons

Heavenly Father, thank You for the seasons of life that shape us. Help me teach my sons to embrace each moment, understanding that You have a purpose for them all. May they find joy in the good times and strength in the challenges, trusting that You are with them every step of the way. Guide us as we navigate these seasons together. Amen.

Add your own personal prayer:

_____
_____
_____
_____
_____
_____
_____
_____
_____
_____
_____
_____
_____
_____
_____
_____
_____
_____
_____
_____
_____

Gardening:
Plant flowers or vegetables together.

As A Boy Mom...

you are blessed with the responsibility of shaping your sons' lives. Jeremiah 29:11 offers a powerful reminder that God has a purpose and a plan for each of them—a plan filled with hope and a bright future. This verse is a comforting truth to share with your boys as they navigate the ups and downs of growing up.

Help your sons understand that God is actively involved in their lives and that He has good plans for them, even when things seem uncertain. Talk about their dreams and encourage them to pursue their passions, reminding them that God delights in their aspirations.

Share your own experiences of how God has guided you through challenges and how His plans often unfold in unexpected ways. Teach them to trust in God's timing, emphasizing that while they may not always see the entire path ahead, they can be assured that God knows what is best for them.

Create a safe family environment that encourages exploration and learning. Celebrate their achievements, big and small, and remind them that each step is part of God's plan. Encourage them to pray about their futures, seeking God's guidance and wisdom in their decisions.

By instilling this understanding, you equip your sons with the confidence to embrace their journey, knowing that God is with them, guiding them toward a hopeful future.

For I know the plans I have for you, declares the Lord, plans for welfare and not for evil, to give you a hope and a future.

Jeremiah 29:11

Praying for my Sons

Dear Lord, thank You for the plans You have for my sons. Help me teach them to trust in Your guidance as they pursue their dreams. May they feel Your presence in their lives, knowing that You are leading them toward a future filled with hope. Strengthen our family as we walk in faith together. Amen.

Add your own personal prayer:

_____
_____
_____
_____
_____
_____
_____
_____
_____
_____
_____
_____
_____
_____
_____
_____
_____
_____
_____
_____
_____
_____
_____

Board Games or Card Games:
Play family favorites or try new ones.

As A Boy Mom...

you experience a whirlwind of emotions and experiences —joy, laughter, challenges, and sometimes frustration. Romans 8:28 offers a comforting promise that God is at work in every aspect of their lives, weaving all things together for good. This truth can provide hope and reassurance in joyful and challenging moments.

Teach your sons that even when things don't go as planned, God has a purpose. Whether they face setbacks in school, conflicts with friends, or the ups and downs of growing up, remind them that God can bring good out of every situation. Help them recognize that challenges can lead to growth, resilience, and deeper faith.

Share personal stories of times when you faced difficulties but later saw how God used those experiences for good. Encourage them to look for the lessons in their own struggles and trust that God's plan is continually unfolding, even if they can't quite see it immediately.

Create an environment where your family can openly discuss life's challenges and victories. Foster gratitude by reflecting on how God has worked in your lives, reminding your boys to look for His goodness in every circumstance.

By instilling this perspective, you equip your sons to navigate life's twists and turns confidently, knowing that God is faithful and working in their lives for their ultimate good.

And we know that for those who love God all things work together for good...

Romans 8:28

Praying for my Sons

Heavenly Father, thank You for the promise that You work all things for good. Help me teach my sons to trust in Your plan, even when they face challenges. May they understand that every experience has purpose and that You are always with them. Strengthen our faith as we walk through life together, recognizing Your goodness in all things. Amen.

Add your own personal prayer:

_____
_____
_____
_____
_____
_____
_____
_____
_____
_____
_____
_____
_____
_____
_____
_____
_____
_____
_____
_____
_____
_____
_____

Make Homemade Pizza: Create personalized pizzas with toppings.

As A Boy Mom...

your heart is often filled with pride and concern as you watch your sons grow and explore the world around them. Psalm 91:11 reassures us of God's protective presence in their lives, reminding us that He commands His angels to guard them in all their ways. This promise can bring peace to any anxious moments you may face as a parent.

Teach your boys about divine protection, helping them understand that they are never alone. Remind them that God's angels are there to watch over them, whether they are playing outside, going to school, or facing new challenges. Encourage them to pray for safety and trust in God's care for them.

Share stories where you felt God's protection or guidance, reinforcing that He is actively involved in their lives. Create a family practice of prayer where you ask for God's protection over one another, emphasizing the importance of relying on Him in all situations.

Encourage open conversations about fears or anxieties they may have. Remind them that it's okay to feel scared sometimes, but they can find comfort in knowing God is always watching over them. Help them to see that their faith can be a source of strength, even when they encounter uncertainty.

By instilling this understanding, you equip your sons with the confidence to face the world boldly, trusting that God's angels are guarding their paths.

For he will command his angels concerning you to guard you in all your ways.

Psalm 91:11

Praying for my Sons

Dear Lord, thank You for Your promise of protection. Help me teach my sons to trust in Your care as they navigate life's adventures. May they feel safe and secure, knowing that You are always watching over them. Strengthen our family as we rely on Your guidance and protection each day. Amen.

Add your own personal prayer:

_____
_____
_____
_____
_____
_____
_____
_____
_____
_____
_____
_____
_____
_____
_____
_____
_____
_____
_____
_____
_____
_____
_____
_____
_____

Painting Rocks: Find rocks and paint them with fun designs.

Discipline your son, for there is hope; do not set your heart on putting him to death.

Proverbs 19:18

As A Boy Mom...

you understand the importance of guidance and discipline in shaping your sons' character. Proverbs 19:18 reminds us that discipline is rooted in love and promises hope for the future. This verse encourages us to embrace the role of a loving guide as we navigate parenting challenges.

Teach your sons that discipline is not merely about correcting behavior but about teaching them valuable life lessons. Encourage them to view discipline as an opportunity for growth rather than punishment. Help them understand that loving discipline helps them develop self-control and wisdom, essential for navigating life's challenges.

Share stories of when you faced the consequences of your actions and how those experiences shaped you into who you are today. This openness fosters trust and encourages your boys to see the value in learning from their mistakes.

Create an environment where discipline is a natural part of your family life. Establish clear expectations and consequences, but always pair them with love and encouragement. Celebrate their successes and remind them that everyone makes mistakes—what matters is how they learn and grow from them.

By instilling this perspective, you equip your sons with the understanding that discipline is a vital part of love and growth, guiding them toward a hopeful and purposeful future.

Praying for my Sons

Heavenly Father, thank You for the gift of discipline and the hope it brings. Help me guide my sons with love and wisdom as they learn and grow. May they understand that discipline is a tool for their development, leading them to become responsible and kind individuals. Strengthen our family as we navigate this journey together. Amen.

Add your own personal prayer:

_____
_____
_____
_____
_____
_____
_____
_____
_____
_____
_____
_____
_____
_____
_____
_____
_____
_____
_____
_____
_____
_____
_____

Bike Riding: Go for a bike ride around the neighborhood.

But he said to me, 'My grace is sufficient for you, for my power is made perfect in weakness...

2 Cor. 12:9

As A Boy Mom...

you may often feel the weight of expectations—both your own and those of others. The parenting journey is filled with moments that can leave you feeling inadequate or overwhelmed. In 2 Corinthians 12:9, Paul reminds us that God's grace is sufficient and His power shines brightest in our weaknesses. This truth can be a source of encouragement for both you and your sons.

Teach your boys that everyone has weaknesses and that it's okay to acknowledge them. Emphasize that these moments of vulnerability provide opportunities for growth and reliance on God. Encourage them to embrace challenges as chances to learn and strengthen their character.

Share your own experiences of feeling weak or unsure and how you turned to God for strength. This openness can help your sons see that it's not about perfection but leaning into God's grace in difficult times. Encourage them to pray and seek God's help when they face challenges, reminding them that His strength is made perfect in their moments of need.

Create a family culture where it's safe to discuss struggles and celebrate perseverance. Help your boys recognize that their weaknesses don't define them; instead, they are part of their journey toward becoming resilient individuals anchored in faith.

By instilling this understanding, you nurture a sense of humility and strength in your sons, empowering them to rely on God in every situation.

Praying for my Sons

Dear Lord, thank You for the gift of Your grace and strength. Help me teach my sons that it's okay to be weak and to rely on You in those moments. May they find comfort in knowing that Your power is made perfect in their vulnerabilities. Strengthen our family as we embrace our weaknesses together and lean on Your grace. Amen.

Add your own personal prayer:

_____
_____
_____
_____
_____
_____
_____
_____
_____
_____
_____
_____
_____
_____
_____
_____
_____
_____
_____
_____
_____
_____

Spa Day at Home: Pamper each other with facials and relaxation.

And he took them in his arms and blessed them, laying his hands on them.

Mark 10:16

As A Boy Mom...

you have a unique opportunity to nurture and shape the hearts of your sons. Mark 10:16 illustrates Jesus' love for children, showing us the importance of embracing and blessing the young ones in our lives. This verse serves as a reminder of the impact your love and attention has on their spiritual and emotional growth.

Teach your boys the value of love and kindness by modeling these qualities. Just as Jesus took the children in His arms, show them how to embrace others with compassion and warmth. Encourage them to be a source of support for friends and those who feel left out or alone.

Create moments in your daily routine to bless your sons —whether through words of encouragement, or simply spending quality time together. Let them know how precious they are in your eyes and in God's eyes. Reinforce the idea that they are cherished and loved, not just by you but also by their Creator.

Share stories of how small gestures of kindness can make a big difference. Encourage your boys to look for opportunities to bless others, reminding them they can reflect Jesus' love in their actions. This strengthens their character and fosters a sense of community and belonging.

By instilling this understanding, you help your sons grow into compassionate individuals who appreciate the beauty of embracing and blessing those around them.

Praying for my Sons

Heavenly Father, thank You for the gift of my sons. Help me to embrace them with love and bless them daily, just as Jesus did. May they understand their worth and learn to extend kindness to others. Strengthen our family as we reflect Your love in our actions and words. Amen.

Add your own personal prayer:

_____
_____
_____
_____
_____
_____
_____
_____
_____
_____
_____
_____
_____
_____
_____
_____
_____
_____
_____
_____
_____
_____

Visit an Art Gallery: Explore local art exhibitions.

As A Boy Mom...

you have the incredible privilege of nurturing unique individuals created in God's image. Psalm 139:14 reminds us of the beauty and intentionality behind each person's creation. This verse is a powerful affirmation for both you and your sons, encouraging a deep appreciation for who they are.

Help your boys understand that they are wonderfully made, with distinct gifts and talents that reflect God's creativity. Encourage them to celebrate individuality and recognize that their differences make them special. Remind them that God has a purpose for each of their lives and delights in who they are.

Share moments when you've seen their unique qualities shine—whether it's their sense of humor, creativity, or kindness. Reinforce the idea that God designed them just as they are and that they should embrace their strengths while acknowledging areas for growth.

Foster an environment where they feel safe expressing themselves and exploring their interests. Encourage them to pursue their passions, knowing that each step they take is part of God's wonderful plan for their lives. Help them understand that their worth is not based on achievements or comparisons but rooted in the truth that they are God's creation.

By instilling this understanding, you empower your sons to walk confidently in their identities, knowing they are fearfully and wonderfully made.

I praise you, for I am fearfully and wonderfully made. Wonderful are your works; my soul knows it very well.

Psalm 139:14

Praying for my Sons

Dear Lord, thank You for creating my sons so wonderfully. Help me instill in them a sense of worth and purpose as they grow. May they embrace their uniqueness and recognize the beauty in who they are. Strengthen our family as we celebrate Your marvelous works in our lives. Amen.

Add your own personal prayer:

_____
_____
_____
_____
_____
_____
_____
_____
_____
_____
_____
_____
_____
_____
_____
_____
_____
_____
_____
_____
_____

Visit a Farm: Check out local farms or petting zoos.

As A Boy Mom...

you are navigating a world filled with distractions and pressures that can easily pull your sons' focus away from what truly matters. Colossians 3:2 encourages us to set our minds on heavenly things, reminding us that our perspective shapes our actions and attitudes. This verse invites you to guide your boys toward a deeper understanding of their identity and purpose in Christ.

Teach your sons the importance of prioritizing their relationship with God. Help them understand that while school, friendships, and hobbies are important, their ultimate worth and direction come from their faith. Encourage them to seek God's wisdom in their daily lives through prayer, reading Scripture, or engaging in meaningful conversations about faith.

Create intentional moments to discuss what it means to focus on the things above. Share stories of individuals who have made choices based on their faith, illustrating the impact of a Christ-centered mindset. Encourage your boys to dream big and aspire to live lives that reflect God's love and purpose.

Foster an environment where they can explore their interests while keeping their eyes on eternal values. Encourage acts of kindness, service, and compassion, helping them see that their actions can reflect God's heart in the world. By instilling this perspective, you equip your sons to navigate life with a focus on eternal significance, guiding them to become young men of faith seeking God's heart.

Set your minds on things that are above, not on things that are on earth.

Colossians 3:2

Praying for my Sons

Heavenly Father, thank You for the gift of my sons. Help me guide them to set their minds on things above and to seek You in all aspects of their lives. May they grow in faith and purpose, reflecting Your love in everything they do. Strengthen our family as we pursue You together. Amen.

Add your own personal prayer:

_____
_____
_____
_____
_____
_____
_____
_____
_____
_____
_____
_____
_____
_____
_____
_____
_____
_____
_____

Play Catch:
Use a baseball, football, or frisbee.

As A Boy Mom...

you may often find yourself juggling numerous responsibilities and facing various challenges. Philippians 4:6 offers a comforting reminder to replace anxiety with prayer and to trust in God's peace. This verse encourages you and your sons to seek God's presence in every situation, fostering a spirit of reliance on Him.

Teach your boys the importance of prayer when they feel overwhelmed or anxious. Help them understand that God cares deeply about their concerns, whether big or small. Encourage them to share their worries with God, knowing He is always listening and ready to provide comfort and guidance.

Create a family practice of prayer, where you regularly gather to express gratitude for God's blessings and raise your concerns. This strengthens your relationship with Him and builds a supportive environment where your boys feel safe sharing their thoughts and feelings.

Share stories of times when prayer brought you peace during challenging moments. Reinforce the idea that God's peace is not dependent on circumstances but a gift available to those who trust Him. Encourage your sons to cultivate a habit of gratitude, helping them focus on the positives in their lives, even amid challenges. By instilling this understanding, you empower your sons to confidently approach life's uncertainties, knowing they can always find peace in God through prayer.

Do not be anxious about anything, but in everything by prayer and supplication with thanksgiving let your requests be made known unto God.

Phil 4:6

Praying for my Sons

Dear Lord, thank You for the gift of prayer and the peace You provide. Help me teach my sons to turn to You in times of anxiety and to trust in Your promises. May our family grow closer as we seek Your presence together. Fill our hearts with Your peace that guards us in Christ Jesus. Amen.

Add your own personal prayer:

_____
_____
_____
_____
_____
_____
_____
_____
_____
_____
_____
_____
_____
_____
_____
_____
_____
_____
_____
_____
_____

Visit a museum: Explore a local museum or science center.

The Lord is my shepherd; I shall not want.

Psalm 23:1

As A Boy Mom...

you have the privilege of guiding and nurturing your sons through life's ups and downs. Psalm 23:1 beautifully captures the essence of God's care for us, reminding us that He is our Shepherd, providing for our needs and leading us with love. This verse offers a comforting truth you can share with your boys as they navigate their journeys.

Help your sons understand what it means to have God as their Shepherd. Just as a shepherd guides and protects his sheep, God watches over them and provides everything they need. Encourage them to trust in God's provision, reminding them that they can rely on Him in every situation, whether they face challenges at school, in friendships, or within themselves.

Create opportunities to discuss how God meets their needs. Share stories from your own life when you experienced God's guidance and provision. Emphasize the importance of faith in trusting that God knows what is best for them, even when circumstances seem difficult.

Encourage your boys to look for ways they can be shepherds to others—offering kindness, support, and friendship to those around them. By modeling and practicing compassion, they can reflect the love of their Shepherd in their daily lives.

By instilling this understanding, you help your sons develop a deep sense of security and trust in God's care, equipping them to face life's challenges with confidence.

Praying for my Sons

Heavenly Father, thank You for being our Shepherd and for providing for our every need. Help me teach my sons to trust in You and to recognize Your guiding hand in their lives. May they find comfort in knowing that they are never alone and that You are always there to lead and protect them. Strengthen our family as we grow in faith together. Amen.

Add your own personal prayer:

_____
_____
_____
_____
_____
_____
_____
_____
_____
_____
_____
_____
_____
_____
_____
_____
_____
_____
_____
_____
_____
_____
_____

Movie night:
Pick a movie, make popcorn, and enjoy a cozy night in.

As A Boy Mom...

you have a unique opportunity to foster a vibrant and genuine faith in your sons. In Luke 18:16, Jesus emphasizes the importance of children in His kingdom, inviting them to come to Him freely. This verse reminds you of the value and significance of your role in nurturing their spiritual lives.

Help your boys understand that they are cherished and important in God's eyes. Encourage them to approach God with the same curiosity and openness children naturally possess. Create an environment where they feel comfortable asking questions about faith, expressing their thoughts, and exploring their relationship with God.

Share Bible stories highlighting God's love for children and His desire for them to know Him. Encourage your sons to see prayer and worship as rituals and opportunities to connect with their Creator personally.

Emphasize the importance of community and fellowship, encouraging them to build friendships with other believers. Help them understand that being part of a faith community can enrich their spiritual journey and provide support as they grow.

By instilling this understanding, you empower your sons to embrace their faith with confidence and joy, knowing they are welcomed into God's kingdom.

But Jesus called them to him, saying, 'Let the children come to me, and do not hinder them...

Luke
18:16

Praying for my Sons

Dear Lord, thank You for welcoming children into Your kingdom. Help me nurture my sons' faith and encourage them to come to You with open hearts. May they understand their value in Your eyes and grow in their relationship with You. Strengthen our family as we walk together in faith. Amen.

Add your own personal prayer:

_____
_____
_____
_____
_____
_____
_____
_____
_____
_____
_____
_____
_____
_____
_____
_____
_____
_____
_____
_____
_____
_____

Bake Cookies: make and decorate cookies together.

As A Boy Mom...

your influence on your sons is profound and lasting. Proverbs 31:28 highlights the beauty of a mother's love and the deep respect her children have for her. This verse serves as a reminder of the legacy you are building through your nurturing, guidance, and unconditional love.

Encourage your boys to recognize the value of expressing gratitude and appreciation. Teach them that words of affirmation can uplift and strengthen relationships. Whether it's a simple "thank you" or a thoughtful note, help them understand the power of acknowledging the efforts and sacrifices you make for them.

Create moments in your daily life to share experiences and memories, reinforcing the bond between you and your sons. Share with them the importance of kindness and respect, not just toward you but others. By modeling these values, you're teaching them how to honor and appreciate the people in their lives.

As they grow, encourage your boys to reflect on the lessons you've taught them about love, resilience, and faith. Inspire them to carry these lessons into their relationships, fostering a cycle of respect and appreciation beyond your family.

By instilling this understanding, you help your sons recognize the blessings of family and the importance of cherishing one another.

Her children rise up and call her blessed; her husband also, and he praises her.

Proverbs 31:28

Praying for my Sons

Heavenly Father, thank You for the gift of being a mother. Help me to nurture my sons with love and wisdom, and may they rise up to call me blessed. Teach us all to appreciate one another and to express our gratitude. Strengthen our family bond as we grow together in love and faith. Amen.

Add your own personal prayer:

_____
_____
_____
_____
_____
_____
_____
_____
_____
_____
_____
_____
_____
_____
_____
_____
_____
_____
_____
_____
_____
_____
_____
_____

Arts and Crafts: make DIY crafts with supplies at home.

Let no one despise you for your youth, but set the believers an example in speech, in conduct, in love, in faith, in purity.

1 Timothy 4:12

As A Boy Mom...

you have an excellent opportunity to shape the character and faith of your sons. In 1 Timothy 4:12, Paul encourages Timothy to be an example despite his youth, reminding us that age does not determine the impact we can have on others. This verse invites you to instill in your boys the importance of living out their faith authentically.

Encourage your sons to embrace their unique gifts and recognize that they can make a difference in the world, no matter their age. Help them understand that their words and actions speak loudly about their beliefs. Teach them the value of integrity, kindness, and compassion in their daily interactions.

Model for them what it means to live a life of faith. Share your own experiences of trusting God and the lessons you've learned along the way. Encourage them to take initiative in their spiritual journey through prayer, serving others, or engaging in discussions about faith.

Create an environment where they feel empowered to express their thoughts and questions about God. Celebrate their growth and encourage them to pursue purity in their hearts and minds, reminding them that these choices reflect their commitment to Christ.

By fostering this understanding, you equip your sons to be confident leaders in their faith, inspiring others through their example.

Praying for my Sons

Dear Lord, thank You for the privilege of being a mother to my sons. Help me guide them to be examples of faith and love in their lives. May they embrace their youth as an opportunity to shine Your light and inspire others. Strengthen our family as we grow together in faith and character. Amen.

Add your own personal prayer:

_____
_____
_____
_____
_____
_____
_____
_____
_____
_____
_____
_____
_____
_____
_____
_____
_____
_____
_____
_____
_____
_____
_____

nature Walks:
Explore local parks or nature trails.